Love, Interrupted

Poems

by Dana C. Barajas

Love, Interrupted

Cover Design: Dana Barajas

LCCN: 2 0 2 5 9 1 4 6 2 2

ISBN 979-8-218-73350-6

Printed in the United States of America

Dedications

For my family
Thank you for loving me as your Donnie. I love you.
Please read with caution.

For Zach
In a burning room, I would still see you.
Rest in peace.

For my younger and future self
This too shall pass.

Contents

Introduction

Dear reader
Since love is an act of violence,
a tale as old as time,
I'll take you back
to a time I thought I was in love.

See, there were many times
I gave my heart
to boys with trust,
but love was a bust.

So now I sit
and write poetry just because.

I hope a piece of me
sticks with you forever,
since you still have my sweater.

I'll meet you in warmer weather,
maybe then you'll make me your Heather.

Haha, clever,
but I told you
never say never.

CHAPTER ONE

Denial

Forget Me Not

I've seen you at your worst,
and you love her now,
but I loved you first.

Dressed in all black
as you lay there in your hearse.

Dear soldier,
I loved you first.

Frank Ocean Eyes

I liked you
because your freckles matched mine.
I liked you
since our first time.
I liked you
when you pulled away,
looked down at me,
and said you couldn't stay.

I looked back
with tears in my eyes.
I swore in that moment
you were feeding me lies.

But it was true.
Monday came,
and a call from you never came through.

Blind Faith

I was wicked
when I lost my way.

You found me
on that narrow road,
drifting further astray.

You tugged—
pulled me back in.
No wonder I fell for you
on a whim.

Telling you my deepest secrets,
my only friend.

You made me feel holy,
like the pain might fade
if you just hold me.

But what if that day comes,
and you miss
the old me?

Fairmont Square Cinema

I remember our first date:
I'll pick you up before 8.

Movies.
I was clueless.

The truth is,
I would marry you tomorrow.

Happenstance

Finding you again
after all those years,
the time,
the distance,
made me realize:

I never outgrew you,
I just never knew you.

Cannabinoid Water

I saw it in glimpses,
his heart and his soul.

In the way he spoke to his own:
his brother,
his mother with a law degree.

Oh, what he would do for that tree.

"I'll meet you in about an hour,"
he'd say,
standing among the pretty flower.

Midnights and beakers,
rows of Yeezy sneakers.

30th-floor views,
the background hum of the news.

The only time
I wasn't afraid to drink liquor.

I just wanted
to be your *it* girl.

Filo

He was seventeen,
so full of light,
gone too soon
under a December sky.

We lost a brother,
she lost her world.
Her second son,
her baby boy curled.

She whispers *Raphael*
into the air,
hoping *Filo*
might still be there.

The house is quiet,
but love remains,
in photos,
in dreams,
and his name.

CHAPTER TWO

Anger

Daddy Issues Barbie

I used to wish he would die,
because every word he said was a lie.

Daddy Issues Barbie.

And my aunts knew.
They knew the affair was true.
Some even helped him too.

Daddy Issues Barbie.

His wife,
a ride-or-die bitch,
'til death do them part.

Now their daughter's
turning the pain into art.

Daddy Issues Barbie.

Ego Death

You're so vain,
I bet you think
these poems are about you.
Don't you?

Blurred Lines

Blurred lines.
We crossed 'em.

Fuck my feelings?
Fuck your feelings.
You can't just toss them.

Treating me like a hoe,
but before
I was your bro.

Now I hate you,
because I'm trying to find peace.

No.
The fuck it wasn't
"just temporary relief."

Death by Betrayal

I call her Judas,
because she ruined us.

We looked like a painting,
the two of us.

I thought we had each other,
even when the world was through with us.

Now what's new with us?
You ruined us, Judas.

Because the only thing I want now
is to fight you.

My feelings are valid.
I have the right to.

I know you think you won,
but you haven't.
I'll get the last laugh in.

Petty Vendettas

Let's settle the score.
You ready?
Ready for more?

Your brother,
I still adore.
He's less of a bore.

You,
you're more of a whore.

I used to happily do every chore,
but you,
you always wanted more,
more,
more,
'til there was nothing left.

You should've killed me instead.

Tony Montana Wannabe

He has a God complex,
but no God in him.

Thinks he's the shit,
because he fucks a lot of women.

You're not hard,
you wouldn't survive in prison.

Always got other men
riding on the tails of your coat.

Please.
You're the furthest thing from a GOAT.

Built on lies,
you can't stay afloat.

All that dick riding
gets old.

You cheated and cheated.
Every empire ends—yours deleted.

Insult to Injury

Let's get this straight:
those stones you throw,
they carry weight.

Those words only hurt
because they come from you,
because I deem them true
if you do.

Without Consent

Everyone was going to rape me that night.
My boyfriend saved me...
then he raped me.

Bars and alcohol.
You knew what I was on,
didn't you, A-A-RON?

Twin Sinners

Two sisters.
One flask.
Four faces.

Smiles in daylight,
knives in dark places.

They toast to love,
then twist the blade.

Betrayal.
Aged and homemade.

Lake Placid

We grew up
on dead-end streets
and borrowed time,
where gossip bloomed
like kudzu vines.

We passed our promises
through porchlight hush,
in a town too quiet
to ever trust.

Shhhhh...

Smiles in public,
daggers in text.
Everyone's loyal,
until you're next.

Feelings Harder Than Your Dick

My feelings hit harder
than your dick ever did.

CHAPTER THREE

Bargaining

Twin Flame

A rosary used to cover his arm,
now a skull is his lucky charm.

I love you.
You say we're not compatible,
that it's unfathomable,
unimaginable.

But in my eyes, you're magical, like a magnet,
so attractable.

Wish I could go back to our bowling days,
before my staring gaze,
before the drug days,
before the mental phase.

I would have read you sooner,
read the stars and the lunar.
Maybe I could've seen it then.

After all,
you were my friend.

Pray Your Name

Who do I pray to about you,
when the prayers never go through?

Looking for my forever,
but always settling
for Mr. Whatever's nevers,
or the
"you could do better's,"

while you're over there
kissing all the Heathers.

Cop Out

Who protects me
when you're gone?
What if it all goes wrong?
What if I lose my mind?

You were the peace
I was never meant to find.

How can you leave first?
That's not the deal,
not how it's supposed to be.

The only cop
I ever called cool.

God,
you beautiful fucking fool.

You didn't even see me bleed.
But I get it.
You've got a mouth to feed.

Stay safe out there on the road.
Call me someday
when we're old.

We both know,
I never had the courage.

Scarlet Love Letter

I didn't beg,
I just wrote you a card instead.

Maybe it's next to your bed,
or maybe you hide it
and read it in your head instead.

I never wished her dead,
I just wished you loved me instead.

We could've painted that town red,
but they would've wanted my head.

Like *Where's Waldo?*
I hated that shirt,
but wearing it...
a subtle way to flirt.

Jealousy: The Eulogy

I'm jealous of her,
she got to read your eulogy.

A church full of people
who never heard of me.

How'd you go from her to me?

They felt for her,
the blonde fiancée
who lost her husband-to-be,
the one who died
overseas.

I'm jealous of her,
she got to read your eulogy.

Screaming Infidelities

Our burning streak ended
on day 104,
wandering eyes
over the Potomac River shore.

How'd we go from that
to this?

You even told me
you saw me having your kids.

I loved him too,
but you were my first pick.

Now you're gone,
because I showed you
I truly am sick?

I guess it's fair
for you to leave
the second you see me bleed.

But now you've reopened a deep cut,
heartbreak.

Mile 0

If I could take you back
to the Florida Keys,
room 619...
what would we ask the queen?
What did she see?

That secret?
Let's keep it between you and me.

Everything I did,
I did for us.
A heart so big,
I thought it would combust.

Fuck the strong feelings.
I just wanted your trust.

But you had to love other girls,
in your mind it was a must.

I cried out loud,
"What about us?"

You laughed it off.

Love?
What the fuck is the rush?

No Rhyme or Reason

This poem lives in my phone.
You live in my phone.

I never want you to feel alone,
so I'll phone you,
beg you to come home soon.

But I know you,
angry at the world,
because your father disowned you.

Mine disowned me too,
something we both went through.

Lavoy

He's two years older,
bolder,
a soldier.

I still remember him
in that blue Hollister polo.

Loved him back
when I was sober,
reconnected
when we were older.

His face, my mom remembered
when I told her.

When I see him,
I'll try and keep my composure.

I look at my phone between texts,
waiting for the time to fly.

Did I finally find the right guy?

Josh in Cursive

She's sweet,
sure.

But she's not the song
you danced to in seventh grade.

Not the girl
who knew your laugh
before your voice changed.

So no.
I don't hope it works out.

I hope you look at her
and feel
everything
you lost.

Let her down easy,
then come home to Florida.

Cocaine Catalyst

I watch you draw
your line of dust,
like it's the only truth
you trust.

And still,
I stay,
hoping love
might be
enough
someday.

I Almost Hate You

But almost
is still love.

The Squeeze (Unanswered)

He used to ask me
if the juice was worth the squeeze.

I never knew how to answer.
Because with you,
it was always bruises,
never sweetness.

CHAPTER FOUR

Depression

Love, Interrupted

I write these words heavily,
a man of service
called to duty.

Grief,
love,
nothing new to me.

We were supposed to make art,
just *you* and *me*.

In loving memory,
across your eulogy.

Anhedonia

Depression again.
Feeling hopeless,
and my mom's yelling again,
like I chose this.

Just focus.
Focus.

The pitter-patter in my brain
is driving me insane.

How can a man
have such power over me?

Every time,
I give them more of me,
'til it's all for free.

And these other boys
I don't even like
keep calling me.

A Day to Remember

I sat in a back-row pew
and listened to them talk.

Stories from your best friends,
you were their rock.

A poem from your mom
about her warrior son.

Fun memories from your dad,
but I knew you when you were sad.

I knew the depression,
the pain behind the tears.

The daddy issues
we both shared over the years.

I knew your fears.

In a back-row pew,
wondering if you see me here.

Montero

I feel you drifting,
vacant texts,
energy shifting.

You'll be in the clouds one day,
but will I be missing?

I regret I didn't kiss you.
I regret it more
when I start to miss you.

You'll always be my mother's choice...
just know
our goodbye
was ultimately your choice.

P.S.
I truly am happy for you.

Sad Beautiful Tragic

How can someone so pretty
be so suicidal?

So pretty,
but never worth the while.

Read between the lines,
look past my smile.

They never love *all* of me,
only parts of me,
the parts that look pretty.

Wifey

You deserve a healthy wife,
not one who runs a knife
up and down her spine
from time to time.

Happy wife,
happy life.

Emo Girl

After the breakup I realize
how much I lack motivation,
stuck in starvation,
smoke to numb the frustrations,
looking for the next...

Maybe a blue-eyed boy
to be my salvation.

Not Bonnie

I'm suicidal.
I can't be a bride.
Not what he pictured
when he thought *Bonnie* and *Clyde*.

I get it.
It's a scary thing to picture:

how my pretty face is a façade
how one day you could be kissing me...
and the next
you could find me
hanging from a shower rod.

BPD

Borderline interlude,
suicidal thoughts ensue.

Still, I miss you.
Wish I would've kissed you.

104 days,
that's all it took
for you to run away.

One hundred and four days.

Poetic Pain

You love to watch me bleed.

One day you'll say,
"It's too much for me."

But for now,
I'm your muse.
To fuck.
To use.
To bruise.

Cory's Room

You know nothing about me
outside of the bedroom.
Maybe you'll see my bigger picture
when I'm dead soon.

But whose room?
Our romance came
and left too soon.
But whose room?
Mine,
or yours?

It's Giving Fuck Boy

We were casual
in the most damaging way.
You needed someone to stay,
and I never knew how to play.

You call me manic,
think I'm schizophrenic.
But when your support system runs dry,
I'm the one you call in a panic.

The back and forth,
he loves me,
he loves me not,
I can't stand it.

It's like we both fear goodbye,
because neither of us knows
how the other will handle it.

Both ends of our candle lit.

Manic Child

I'm a lot of things
you'll never get to see.

Little ol' me,
the baby of the family tree.
Too loyal to ever leave,
a giver of love for free,
future mother of three.

Yeah, I'm a lot of things
you'll never get to see.

Too wrapped up
in your smoke and apathy.

Yeah, I'm a lot of things
you'll never get to see.

The Shy Fuck

I used to be shy to undress.
Felt like no man
I could impress.
With these tiny tits
and small ass,
I swore they used me
for time to pass.
So I'd fuck 'em once,
then who's next?

Not him.
He's just a friend.

Down Bad

I did it again.
Fell in love with a man.
Told him he was my only friend.

Didn't fuck him.
Now he's gone.
Again?
What'd I do wrong?

He told me
the feelings he had were strong.

What was my crime?
We talked all the time.

I'M C R A Z Y.
He read between the lines.

In the Name of Being Honest

You loved me
'til you didn't.

Mr. Committed.

That night on the phone
you said you'd stay alive for me.

In my vision
I saw a crash over the sea.

Still,
she was your bride-to-be.

Because truth be told,
you loved her
more
than me.

Foe of Mine

Did you ever really care
or were you just there?

I didn't think you deserved
a page of your own.
Because God knows
if I wrote you a poem,
you'd use it against me,
judging from your invisible throne.

You'd twist my words,
try to make out the meaning.

But it doesn't matter.
I'm still the one bleeding.

Lucky Seven

Seven siblings,
one broken man.

Rage in his fist,
a bottle in hand.

But mama
stitched peace
into every cracked wall,
loved us loud
when he loved
not at all.

Medical Melodies

I take my pills
like prayers,
washed down
with lyrics
that almost
understand me.

It doesn't cure it,
but some days
the ache learns how to sing.

It sings like Lana Del Rey,
Cinnamon Girl on replay.

CHAPTER FIVE

Acceptance

To All the Boys

Thank you
to every boy I loved along the way.

The ones who left.
The ones who lingered.
The ones who fixed me.
The ones who broke me.
The ones who wouldn't play.

The curly-haired.
The unlucky.
The self-made.
The ones whose stare
turned me to stone.

I'm on my way,
forever alone.

Thank Me Later

You'll silently thank me one day
for knowing we both deserved better,
even if that meant
not being together.

But sometimes I wonder
who were you
before the world made you cold?
Before you grew old?

Before they shattered your dreams
while you were still sleeping.
Before other lovers
left you weeping.

Womanhood

Dating in your 30s,
shit gets discouraging.

Get married.
Have a baby.
They beat it in my brain
with such urgency.

Shit, I'm barely flourishing.

And what about a father?
Shouldn't I find someone
who's at least *a bit* nurturing?

It's easy, I'm sure you think.
But the truth I'll tell you
bleeds past the ink.

I've never desired
to paint a room pink
or blue, for that matter.

Until you.

And I'll tell you the truth:
I'd paint every wall
every shade of blue.
I'd do it for you.

Radical Acceptance

I used to think money
could solve all my issues.

The paper I really needed
was some tissue.

The men drove me mad.
My shallow friends made me sad.

Truth is,
I should've taken my own advice.
Therapy ain't that bad.

Hopeful Lullabies

Someday maybe
it won't hurt so much.

Someday,
when I'm older maybe.

Someday maybe
I'll be a mother,
watch over a baby boy
and his brother.

Maybe I'll be good,
God'll gift me another,
a baby girl.

The Weed Awakening

He smoked himself sober,
choking on thoughts
of growing older.

Retired Love

The love I had
is down to nothing.

I was young.
I was dumb.
I was wrong.
You were never the one.

I'm sorry it took six years.
I'm sorry for all the tears.
I'm sorry I couldn't stay,
a price we both must pay.

I'll love you forever,
but forever wasn't long enough.
I tried to make it to the afterlife,
but our bond wasn't strong enough.

You made me lose myself in the fight.
Maybe my fault
for always needing to be right.

I hope you find the one,
someone who sees you as the sun,
so you can finally shine bright.

And maybe then
you'll understand
I was right.

She/Her They/Them

They go by She and They.
For the first time
I feel a little gay.
Not all the way,
just a little gay.
Because blue
is the color of you.
You see,
my name was supposed to be Ashley too.
And the girl at Starbucks
told me I looked like you.

So I smiled
and said nothing,
because some feelings
don't ask to be spoken,
they just bloom quietly
and break you open.

Toxic Little Comfort Character

You have good memories of me
to soften the sting of the bad,
and that's why
you can't let go.

I have no good ones, only bad,
and that's why
I can't hold on.

There's nothing to latch on.

You say you love your mother,
but can't stay sober
long enough
to hold her.

One morning I woke up
and finally knew
what I was never
sure of with you,
my toxic little comfort character.

The Daughter and Sister You Kept

I warned them
I'm not always light.

Some days
I vanish
beneath my own mind.

But they stayed.
Not to save me,
just to sit
beside the dark.

I Met Her in Melbourne

I lost her, but I found you,
through a friend we both once knew.
Sippin' Corona, salt and lime,
felt like I met you in some other life.

Both Sagittarius, written in the stars,
a year minus six days apart,
and your face looked like art.
I wondered how we were ever apart.

Like Kelso, I think of Jackie now and then,
and I'm right back in Melbourne again.

Mission Complete

My mom said
your mission here on Earth is complete.
God set you free.

She doesn't know
you're the reason I believe.

I even swore
I'd change my ways.
No more tattoos,
or drug days.

Nevermore

I never got the closure
I kept crying for.

So I built it with my hands,
line by line,
from torn pages
and unsaid words.

I still think of you,
all of you,
but not with longing.

Just breath.
Just space.
Just the quiet that comes
after the storm forgets your name.

If love was interrupted,
then maybe this is the part
where I stop waiting
for it to finish.

Afterword

In early 2023, I reconnected with my middle school sweetheart, the boy who once took me on movie dates and made the long drive to visit during my first year of college. Life had taken us in different directions, but Zach and I always acknowledged the invisible string that had tied us together and led us back to this reunion.

So many memories. So many feelings. So much time to make up for.

As Zach prepared for deployment to Japan, we rekindled our shared love for creating and consuming art through music, poetry, films, and meaningful conversations about philosophy and life. In the process, he even brought me back to my faith.

We communicated through lyrics, through poems, through a deep connection we called being *musical soulmates*. We shared a fierce appreciation for Blink-182 and proudly identified as emo adults; for us, it was never just a phase.

Deployment meant distance, years apart, but still, we dreamed. We planned to write books, songs, and poems. We were going to start a band: *The Urban.*

Somewhere between romantic and platonic, we loved each other. In our own way, fully.

Zach deployed. I kept living.

Then, in November of that year, Zach lost his life in an Osprey military aircraft crash off the coast of Japan, alongside eight other soldiers.

And I lost a piece of myself.

Publishing this collection is both a labor of love and a tribute to Zach, and to the art we never had the chance to create together. There's a quiet beauty in knowing that some of these poems… Zach was the first to ever read.

One hundred angels died crying for you

Transit umbra lux permanet

Acknowledgements

To the artists
You have unknowingly inspired me to create beauty from my own madness. Now I know how putting art into the world feels like ripping your heart out and bleeding out your vulnerabilities for everyone to see. Fuck. Thank you.

To Coleby
When others called me crazy,
you sat with me on the beach, let me feel,
and watched me write. You are my safe space.
I'm forever grateful. I love you.

To the readers
Thank you.